Explore new ideas!

We...
Reading/Writing
Workshop

Read and reread exciting literature or informational texts!

Become an expert writer!

Use what you have learned to unlock the Wonders of reading!

Mc Graw Hill **Education**

Bothell, WA • Chicago, IL • Columbus, OH • New York, NY

(tl) Superstudio/The Image Bank/Getty Images; (ct) Jason Chapman; (cb) Robert Daly/OJO Images/Getty Images; (b) Nathan Love

Cover and Title Pages: Nathan Love

www.mheonline.com/readingwonders

C

The McGraw·Hill Companies

 Education

Copyright © 2014 The McGraw-Hill Companies, Inc.

Send all inquiries to:
McGraw-Hill Education
Two Penn Plaza
New York, New York 10121

4TEXTO0483031%

ISBN: 978-0-02-119652-4
MHID: 0-02-119652-4

Printed in the United States of America.

3 4 5 6 7 8 9 RJE 17 16 15 14 13

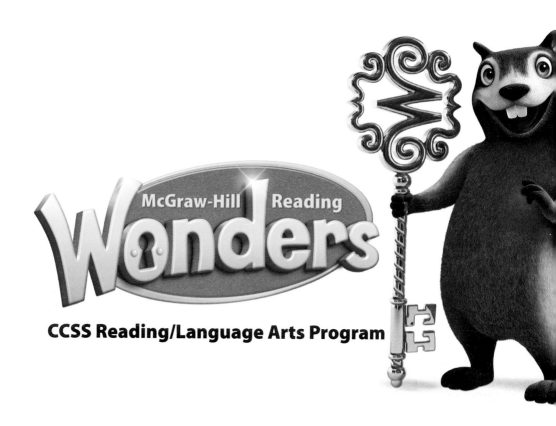

McGraw-Hill Reading Wonders

CCSS Reading/Language Arts Program

Program Authors

Diane August

Donald R. Bear

Janice A. Dole

Jana Echevarria

Douglas Fisher

David Francis

Vicki Gibson

Jan Hasbrouck

Margaret Kilgo

Jay McTighe

Scott G. Paris

Timothy Shanahan

Josefina V. Tinajero

Education

Bothell, WA • Chicago, IL • Columbus, OH • New York, NY

Unit 1

Getting to Know Us

The Big Idea

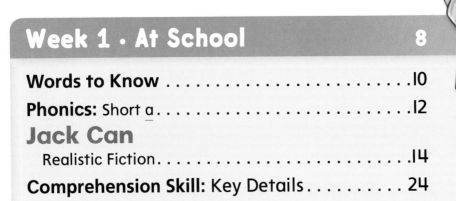

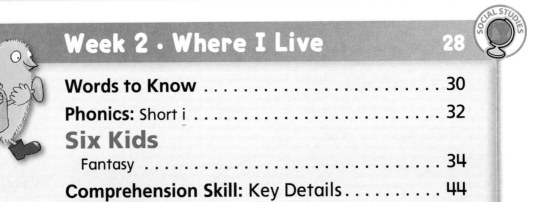

(t) Guy Francis; (b) Jason Chapman

4

Go Digital! www.mheonline.com/readingwonders

Getting to Know Us

Something About Me

There's something about me

That I'm knowing.

There's something about me

That isn't showing.

I'm growing!

The Big Idea

What makes you special?

Essential Question

What do you do at your school?

Go Digital!

Back to School

COLLABORATE

Talk About It

What are these girls doing in school?

does

Dan **does** his best work.

not

Do **not** run at school.

school

We read a lot in **school**.

what

What can we play today?

COLLABORATE

Your Turn

Say the sentence for each word. Then make up another sentence.

Go Digital! Use the online visual glossary

(tl) Blend Images/Getty Images; (bl) Erik Isakson/Getty Images; (tr) Digital Vision/Getty Images; (br) Blend Images/Getty Images

Short a

The letter a can make the short a sound in **pack**.

ax	can	sad
fan	hat	jam
pan	ran	map
tack	back	wag

Nan ran back to the mat.

Nan sat on the mat.

COLLABORATE

Your Turn

Look for these words with short a in "Jack Can."

Jack   **can**   **Max**

sad   **Nan**

Guy Francis

Essential Question

What do you do at your school?

Read about what friends can do at school.

Go Digital!

Guy Francis

14

Max can.

Can Jack? Jack can.

Max can. Can Jack?

Jack can **not**.

Jack is sad.

What does Nan do?

Nan helps Jack!

Jack likes **school**.

Key Details

Key details help you understand a story.

Words and pictures in a story give you the key details.

🔍 Find Text Evidence

Find key details about what Jack can do.

page 17

Can Jack? Jack can.

Detail		Detail		Detail
Jack can make a picture of himself.	→	Jack can not reach.	→	Nan helps Jack reach.

Your Turn

COLLABORATE

Talk about key details in "Jack Can."

Go Digital! Use the interactive graphic organizer

 # Readers to...

Ideas Jan thought about something she did at school. Then she wrote about it.

Jan's Sentences

I can tag Pam.

Pam can tag me.

Your Turn

COLLABORATE

Tell what idea Jan wrote sentences about.

Sachiko Yoshikawa

Writers

Sentences A **sentence** is a group of words that tells a complete thought.

A sentence begins with a capital letter.

I can tag Pam.

Your Turn

- Find another sentence Jan wrote.
- Write new sentences. Circle the capital letter in each sentence.

27

Essential Question

What is it like where you live?

Go Digital!

Outside My Window

Sven Hagolani/Getty Images

Talk About It

What does the boy see outside his window?

down

We go **down** the steps.

out

They go **out** to play.

up

They went **up** the hill.

very

It is **very** loud in the city.

COLLABORATE

Your Turn

Say the sentence for each word. Then make up another sentence.

Go Digital! **Use the online visual glossary**

31

Short i

The letter i can make the short i sound in **six**.

it	is	sit
him	big	dip
kid	pig	lid
sick	kiss	miss

Jason Chapman

Nick ran up a big hill.

Will he sit with Jill?

Your Turn

COLLABORATE

Look for these words with short i in "Six Kids."

six	kids	hill	dig
pick	dip	will	fix it

33

Essential Question

What is it like where you live?

Read about what an animal family does where they live.

Go Digital!

Jason Chapman

Six Kids

Six kids go **out**.

Jason Chapman

Six kids go **up** a hill.

Six kids dig, dig, dig.

Six kids go **down**.

Six kids pick, pick, pick.

Six kids are **very** blue.

Six kids dip, dip, dip.

That will fix it.

Six kids like it here!

Key Details

Key details help you understand a story.

The sequence is the order in which the key details happen.

 Find Text Evidence

Find a key detail about what the six kids do first.

page 37

Six kids (go **up** a hill.)

Detail	Detail	Detail
First six chicks walk up a hill carrying farm tools.	Then they dig holes to plant seeds in their garden.	Then the six chicks pick blueberries.

Go Digital! Use the interactive graphic organizer

Your Turn

COLLABORATE

What happens next? Talk about other key details in "Six Kids."

 Readers to...

Ideas Bill had an idea about a place. He thought of details to describe it.

Bill's Story

Sid is a pig.

He sits on a big hill.

Sid picks six apples.

Your Turn

What details did Bill put in his story to describe a place?

46

Writers

Word Order The **words** in a sentence must be in the correct **order** to make sense.

A telling sentence ends with a period.

He sits on a big hill.

Your Turn

• Find another sentence in Bill's story. Are the words in the correct order?

• Write new telling sentences.

47

Jason Chapman

Essential Question

What makes a pet special?

Go Digital!

48

Special Friends

 Talk About It

What pet do you have or would you like to have?

be

A turtle can **be** a fun pet.

come

My bunny will **come** to eat.

good

A cat is a **good** pet.

pull

I **pull** my dog in a wagon.

Your Turn

COLLABORATE

Say the sentence for each word. Then make up another sentence.

Go Digital! *Use the online visual glossary*

l-blends

The letters bl, cl, fl, gl, pl, and sl make the beginning sounds in **black**, **click**, **flat**, **glad**, **plan**, and **slim**.

flap	slips	flag
glass	blip	clap
class	flips	blab
plans	slick	slam

Our class pet is named Slick.

Slick can flip in its glass bowl!

Your Turn

Look for these words with l-blends in "A Pig for Cliff."

Cliff	glad	Slim
black	slam	slip

Essential Question

What makes a pet special?

Read about Cliff's new pet.

Go Digital!

Constanza Basaluzzo

54

A Pig for Cliff

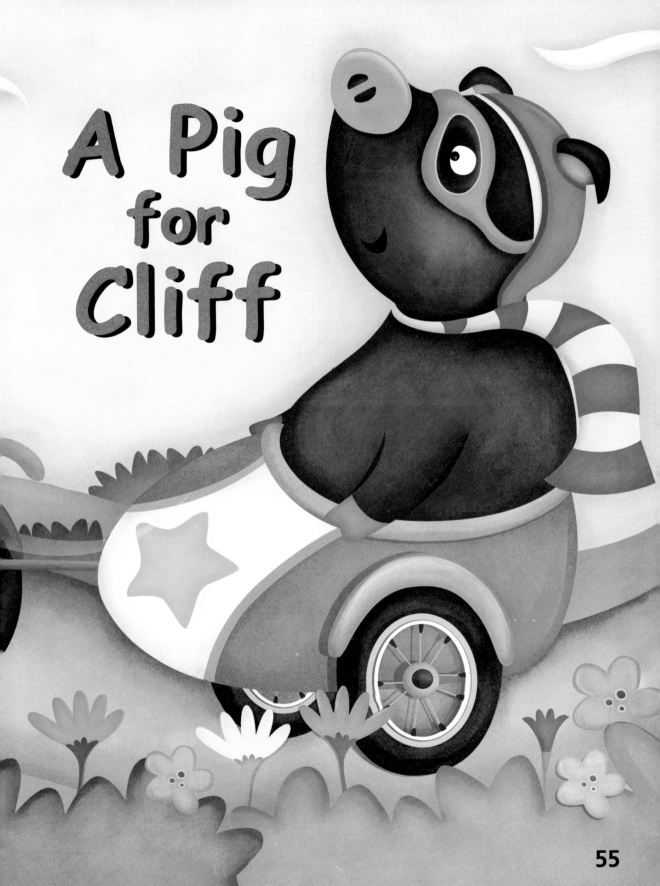

Cliff is glad.

Cliff has a new pet.

It is Slim.

It is a big black pig.

Slim can not fit in!

Come out, Slim!

Slam!

Cliff can not sit with Slim.

Constanza Basaluzzo

Cliff and Slim slip.

Slim can go up.

Cliff can not.

Slim can **pull** Cliff.

Slim will **be** a **good** pet!

Key Details

Key details help you understand a story.

Key details happen in order, or in sequence.

🔍 Find Text Evidence

Find a key detail in the story.

page 57

It is Slim.

It is a big black pig.

Detail	Detail	Detail
Cliff has a big, black pet pig named Slim.	Slim breaks the swing, so Cliff and Slim fall in the mud.	Slim pulls Cliff up out of the mud. Slim is a good pet.

Your Turn

COLLABORATE

Talk about your favorite details in "A Pig for Cliff." Tell about them in order.

Go Digital! Use the interactive graphic organizer

65

Ideas Kim wrote about a silly cat. She used details to describe it.

Kim's Sentences

Bill is quick.

Bill slips and flips.

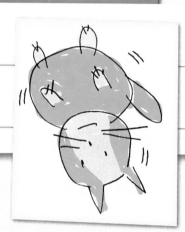

Your Turn

COLLABORATE

Tell what details Kim used to describe her idea.

Constanza Basaluzzo

66

Writers

Statements A **statement** is a sentence that tells something.

A statement ends with a period.

Bill is quick.

Your Turn

- Find another statement that Kim wrote.
- Write new statements. Circle the period at the end.

Weekly Concept Let's Be Friends

Essential Question
What do friends do together?

Go Digital!

Just for Fun

Talk About It

What do you and your friends do together?

fun

It is **fun** to play tag with friends.

make

We can **make** funny hats.

they

Can **they** go up and down fast?

too

We like to skate, **too**!

Your Turn

COLLABORATE

Say the sentence for each word. Then make up another sentence.

Go Digital! *Use the online visual glossary*

Short o

The letter o can make the short o sound in **hop**.

box	top	rocks
not	lot	fox
jog	clock	toss
dolls	hot	mops

Nathan Jarvis

Can Ron jog on a hot day?

Ron can jog a lot!

Your Turn

COLLABORATE

Look for these words with short o in "Toss! Kick! Hop!"

toss   hop   block

dolls   flop

Essential Question

What do friends do together?

Read about how friends play together.

Go Digital!

Toss!
Kick!
Hop!

Kids play together.

Kids zip, zip, zip.

Kids toss, toss, toss.

78

Kids kick, kick, kick, **too**!

Kids **make** block houses.

Kids make dolls.

Kids hop in sacks.

Hop, hop, flop!

They have **fun**!

Key Details

Key **details** tell important information about the selection.

You can use photos to learn key details.

🔍 Find Text Evidence

Find a key detail that tells about one way that friends play together. Use the words and pictures.

page 78

Kids toss, toss, toss.

Corbis Bridge/Alamy

84

Detail		Detail		Detail
Kids toss balls.	⇒	Kids make dolls.	⇒	Kids hop in sacks.

Your Turn

Talk about other key details in "Toss! Kick! Hop!"

Go Digital! Use the interactive graphic organizer

 **Readers to...**

Organization Roz organized her story to compare details.

Roz's Story

Rob and I like to jog a lot!

Does Jon jog, too? He does not!

Jon likes to play with blocks.

 COLLABORATE

Your Turn

Tell what details Roz compared in her story.

Writers

A **question** is a sentence asked to find out something. A question ends with a **question mark**.

An **exclamation** is a sentence that expresses strong feelings. An exclamation ends with an **exclamation mark**.

Does Jon jog, too**?**

He does not**!**

Your Turn

COLLABORATE

- Find another exclamation.
- Write new questions and exclamations.

Nathan Jarvis

Essential Question

How does your body move?

Go Digital!

Robert Houser/UpperCut Images/Getty Images

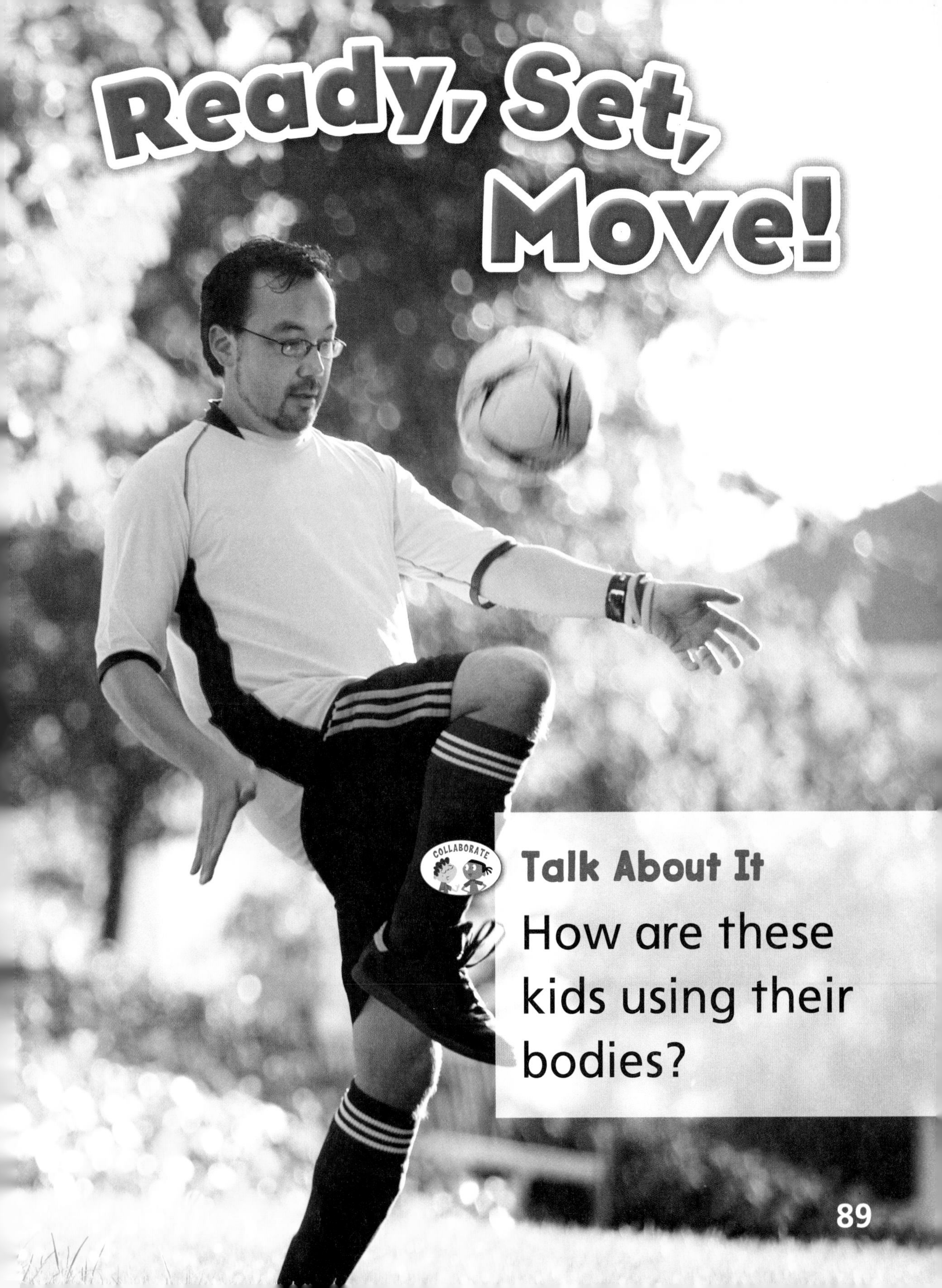

Ready, Set, Move!

COLLABORATE

Talk About It

How are these kids using their bodies?

jump

Do you like to **jump**?

move

It is fun to **move** to music.

run

My dog can **run** fast.

two

The **two** cats like to play.

Your Turn

COLLABORATE

Say the sentence for each word.
Then make up another sentence.

Go Digital! Use the online visual glossary

r-blends, s-blends

The letters br, cr, dr, fr, gr, pr, tr, sk, sm, sn, sp, st, and sw make the beginning sounds in **brick, crab, drip, frog, grass, prop, trap, skin, smack, sniff, spot, still**, and **swam**.

brag   **crib**   **drop**

grab   **swims**   **track**

skips   **snaps**   **stop**

trip   **stick**   **spill**

Fran can run, spin, and skip.

Gram stops to see Fran's trick.

Your Turn

COLLABORATE

Look for these words with r-blends and s-blends in "Move and Grin!"

grin	frog	Scott	
swim	Fran	trot	
Stan	crab	grab	Skip

Essential Question

How does your body move?

Read about how animals and kids move.

Go Digital!

Move and Grin!

Paul van Hoof/ANP Photo/age fotostock

Scott's frog can hop and **jump**.

It can **move** its back legs.

Scott can hop and jump, too.

Hop, hop, jump.

Fran's dog can swim a lot.

It kicks its **two** front legs.

Fran can swim a lot, too.

Swim, swim, swim.

Stan's horse can trot and **run**.

It jogs on its big long legs.

Stan can trot and run, too.

Trot, trot, run.

David Stoecklein/Lithium/Getty Images

Skip's crab can grab.

It can grab with its claw.

Grab, grab, grab.

hand

head

arm

leg

foot

Skip can grab, too.

Grab, grab, grab.

What can Skip grab with?

Key Details

Key details tell important information about the selection.

You can use words and photos to learn key details.

 Find Text Evidence

Find key details that tell how Fran's dog moves. Use the words and pictures.

page 98

Fran's dog can swim a lot.

It kicks its **two** front legs.

First Light/Alamy

Detail		Detail
Fran's dog can swim.	→	It kicks its two front legs.

Your Turn

Talk about the key details in "Move and Grin!"

Go Digital! *Use the interactive graphic organizer*

 # Readers to...

Organization Brad put the events in order in his story about soccer.

Brad's Story

I move the ball on the grass.

Then I kick it into the net.

Did I make a goal?

I did!

Your Turn

Tell the order of events in Brad's story.

Writers

Sentences can be statements, questions, or exclamations.

A sentence begins with a capital letter and ends with a period, a question mark, or an exclamation mark.

I move the ball on the grass.

Your Turn

COLLABORATE

- Find other sentences in Brad's story. Name the end mark used.

- Write new statements, questions, and exclamations. Circle the end mark in each sentence.